CW01500661

Original title:
Journey to the Center

Author: Daisy Dewi
ISBN HARDBACK: 978-1-80561-060-1
ISBN PAPERBACK: 978-1-80561-621-4

Underneath the Veil

Whispers dance in twilight's glow,
Shadows linger, soft and slow.
Secrets wrapped in silken threads,
Dreams are where the heart is fed.

Beneath the stars, a hidden grace,
Time stands still in this sacred space.
Veils of silence softly sigh,
Murmured truths that never die.

Glimmers of light break through the dark,
Echoes linger, a distant spark.
In the hush, the spirits blend,
A timeless song, without an end.

Beneath the Borders

Lands divide, yet hearts remain,
Across the lines, we feel the pain.
Mountains high and rivers wide,
But love knows none, it will not hide.

In quiet towns where echoes play,
Stories whispered day by day.
Underneath the skin we share,
Hope emerges, tender, rare.

Boundaries stand but dreams still soar,
Cultures meet on distant shore.
In shared laughter and gentle tears,
Bridges built to span our fears.

Secrets of the Subsoil

Roots entwined in whispered lore,
Buried tales that yearn for more.
In the dark, life finds its way,
Nurtured thoughts in earthy clay.

Mysteries swirl in dampened earth,
Silent truths await their birth.
Fossils speak of ages past,
Silent witnesses held steadfast.

Beneath our feet, a world unseen,
Underground, where moments glean.
Nature's rhythm, soft, profound,
In subterranean dreams, we're found.

A Survey of the Deep

Waves crash down on ancient stone,
Where the secrets dwell alone.
Vast blue depths, a hidden realm,
Mysteries beyond the helm.

In the silence, whispers roam,
Fish and shadows find their home.
Coral kingdoms rise and fall,
Nature's art, an ocean's call.

Charting depths with quiet grace,
Explorers seek the timeless space.
In the currents, stories weave,
In the deep, we learn to believe.

Arteries of the World

Rivers flow, a silver thread,
Connecting lands where stories spread.
Mountains stand, their heights so bold,
Whispering secrets of the old.

Cities pulse with life and dreams,
Dancing shadows in moonlit beams.
Echoes of laughter fill the air,
As heartbeats linger everywhere.

Highways stretch like veins entangled,
Through valleys deep, where hopes are wrangled.
Each turn reveals a tale untold,
In vibrant hues of red and gold.

Oceans breathe with tides that sway,
While ships drift slowly, lost in play.
In every wave, a journey starts,
A map of dreams within our hearts.

Bound together by the threads,
Of stories whispered, gently led.
Arteries of life, intertwine,
In their embrace, we are divine.

Mapping the Unseen

In shadows deep, where whispers dwell,
Lies a world we cannot tell.
Painted paths on paper drawn,
Guide us gently into dawn.

Through forests thick, where secrets hide,
Nature guards what lies inside.
A flicker here, a glimmer there,
Unseen wonders, breathe the air.

Each corner turned reveals a face,
Of hidden joy, lost in space.
The map unfolds, our hearts ignite,
With every step, we find the light.

Time's ink stains the edges worn,
Of memories cherished, love reborn.
As we wander, we become more,
Mapping truths behind each door.

In the silence, listen keen,
For the echoes of the unseen.
Adventure waits, so take your chance,
In every glance, a sacred dance.

The Depths Await

In emerald depths, where silence sleeps,
The ocean holds its secrets deep.
Waves that crash like time's embrace,
Whisper tales of a hidden place.

Creatures swim in shadows cast,
Where the light fades, depths hold fast.
Coral gardens, a vibrant glow,
In the darkness, life does flow.

Submerged dreams, where treasures lay,
Mermaids sing of lost midday.
Echoes of ships, their stories spin,
In the depths, new worlds begin.

With each dive, the heart takes flight,
Into the blue, past day and night.
The abyss calls with a silent plea,
For those who seek the great, the free.

The depths await, a siren's song,
Calling forth where we belong.
In the stillness, we dare to roam,
Finding our way, we create a home.

Digging for Treasures

In the earth, beneath our feet,
Lies history's pulse, oh so sweet.
With every shovel, stories rise,
Covering paths to ancient skies.

Old coins gleam in the sun's first light,
Fragments of dreams, a joyful sight.
With dusty hands, we search and find,
Lost memories that lie entwined.

Beneath the roots of aging trees,
Lies whispered tales upon the breeze.
Artifacts of what has been,
Unraveling time's forgotten skin.

Amidst the dirt, we unearth gold,
Silent whispers of the bold.
Echoes linger, tales unfurl,
In every find, a hidden world.

So dig we must, through time and space,
For every treasure holds a trace.
And in each moment, lives concealed,
A legacy that won't be healed.

The Earth's Unfolding

Beneath the sky, the fields do sway,
Life emerges from the clay.
Whispers of the wind, they call,
Nature's beauty, free for all.

Mountains rise with grace and might,
Casting shadows, holding light.
Rivers carve a path so bold,
Tales of ancient stories told.

Leaves that dance in golden hues,
Morning's dew, a sparkling muse.
The seasons shift, they ebb and flow,
In every corner, life will grow.

From the roots, the flowers bloom,
A tapestry through sun and gloom.
Sky and soil, a sacred bond,
In this realm, we all respond.

So cherish well the earth's embrace,
In every leaf, find quiet grace.
A journey shared, a bond profound,
In the unfolding, joy is found.

Exploring What Lies Below

In silence deep, the secrets lie,
Where shadows breathe, and echoes sigh.
Roots entwined in earth's embrace,
Hidden worlds, a sacred space.

Through tunnels dark, we wander slow,
Curious hearts where waters flow.
Specters of the past emerge,
Whispers soft, a gentle surge.

Minerals gleam in twilight's glow,
Nature's treasures, row by row.
Caves that sing with voices pure,
Harmony in shadows, sure.

Life takes flight in varying form,
In darkness blooms a hidden norm.
Journey deep to find the light,
Emerging strong from depths of night.

So, let us seek what may not show,
The diamond's glint beneath the snow.
What lies below, a world divine,
In roots and stone, our hearts align.

Through Root and Stone

A journey starts in roots so low,
Beneath our feet, life's stories flow.
Time weaves through these ancient strands,
Nature's art in sculpted lands.

Stone and earth, a strong embrace,
Holding time in every place.
Through the cracks, the greenest sprout,
Whispers soft of life throughout.

Seasons change, the colors blend,
Each cycle brings a new ascend.
From the shadows, life will rise,
Miracles in every guise.

With each step, we tread with care,
Honoring roots both rich and rare.
In the stillness, hear the tone,
Our connection through root and stone.

A universe within the ground,
In simple sights, let joy abound.
Embrace the path, the wild unknown,
Together, we are never alone.

A Dance with Depth

In ocean's heart, the silence sings,
Depths conceal the world's great things.
Tides that pull with gentle grace,
Under waves, a hidden place.

Sunlight filters through the swell,
In every wave, there's magic, tell.
Creatures glide where shadows dwell,
In the quiet, we rebel.

Coral cities breathe and thrive,
In each crack, the pulse alive.
Anemones sway with soft embrace,
In this dance, we find our space.

Beneath the surface, mysteries lay,
In the blue, we dream and play.
A journey wrapped in liquid grace,
In the depths, we find our place.

So dive into the deep unknown,
Embrace the waves, let currents own.
In the dance with depth, we're free,
In every wave, our souls agree.

The Unseen Tapestry

Threads intertwined, colors blend,
A tale of lives, on earth they penned.
Silent whispers in every seam,
A woven path, the unseen dream.

In shadows cast by hopes and fears,
Each stitch holds laughter, love, and tears.
Beneath the surface, stories thrive,
Tales of the heart, forever alive.

Patterns change with every tide,
In this tapestry, we confide.
Fingers tracing where we've been,
The unseen ties that bind within.

Fabric dances in softest light,
A myriad of day and night.
Life's quiet moments, art's embrace,
Unraveling time with gentle grace.

In every fold, a memory lost,
The tapestry reveals its cost.
But still it grows, with every breath,
A living tale that conquers death.

In the Quiet Depths

Beneath the waves, where silence reigns,
Hidden secrets, forgotten chains.
Gentle currents, soft and slow,
Whispers of life, where dreams can flow.

Shadows dance in depths below,
Ancient echoes, stories glow.
Where creatures roam, and silence sings,
In the quiet, a comfort brings.

Time drifts slowly, like a stream,
In these depths, we find a dream.
Mysteries wrapped in blue embrace,
Nature's canvas, a tranquil space.

Light filters down, a gentle touch,
Illuminating what means so much.
In the depths, the heart can find,
Peaceful moments, unconfined.

In stillness grows a vibrant tale,
A sanctuary, a soothing veil.
Under the waves, life in full view,
In the quiet depths, we renew.

Stories Hidden in Soil

Whispers beneath the fertile ground,
Ancient tales waiting to be found.
Roots entwined in a dance of time,
Living memories, ripe for rhyme.

Nurtured by rain, kissed by the sun,
Each grain of earth holds stories spun.
In silent layers, life unfolds,
A library of secrets, whispered golds.

The pulse of life, the heart of clay,
These hidden tales bloom every day.
Buried treasures beneath our feet,
In soil's embrace, the past we meet.

Time unfurls as the seasons change,
Every harvest, a story strange.
In every plot, we sow our fears,
In the soil's warmth, we find our tears.

A tapestry woven through nature's hand,
Where stories linger, forever stand.
In the earth's cradle, we all belong,
In hidden stories, we find our song.

Where Secrets Lie

In the corners of a silent room,
Whispers linger, shadows loom.
Behind closed doors, the heart will spy,
The gentle places where secrets lie.

In quiet moments, truth will wane,
A fragile thread, a tethered chain.
What's left unspoken, held so tight,
Shimmers like stars in the endless night.

Underneath the surface, calm and bright,
Lurk the stories lost to light.
Veiled in hope, the silence cries,
In hushed tones, where the heart complies.

Behind the smiles, in every sigh,
Echoes of things we often deny.
In the heart's chamber, the shadows sigh,
Unveiling tales where secrets lie.

From whispered dreams, to silent pleas,
In the hush, the heart's unease.
Gathered here, we learn to try,
To embrace the truths where secrets lie.

Beneath the Surface

In shadows deep, secrets lie,
Whispers echo, softly sigh.
Ripples dance on tranquil seas,
Unseen depths, a world to seize.

Silent currents pull me down,
Where lost treasures wear a crown.
The heart of ocean, cold and blue,
Hides the dreams that flow anew.

Bubbles rise, a fleeting trace,
Of stories told in liquid space.
A realm of wonders, dark yet bright,
Beneath the surface, life takes flight.

Coral gardens, vibrant bloom,
Exotic creatures, free from gloom.
In this ballet, I am drawn,
Where life awakens with the dawn.

So deep I dive, with gentle grace,
To find my place in this embrace.
Beneath the surface, I explore,
The silent world, forevermore.

Voyage to the Core

Set sail on waves of fate,
Navigating paths ornate.
With compass true, I steer my way,
Into the depths where shadows play.

The roaring sea beneath my craft,
Holds mysteries, whispers soft and shaft.
Guided by stars, I roam the night,
Seeking the heart, the lost light.

Layers thick, a world unknown,
Every heartbeat, every tone.
I voyage forth, with spirit bold,
To find the treasures yet untold.

Through tempests fierce and winds that wail,
I press on with my weary sail.
The core awaits, a promise bright,
In every pulse of day and night.

As depths unfold their ancient lore,
I grasp the truth forevermore.
A voyage that shall never cease,
To find the core, my soul's release.

Explorations Within

In quiet rooms of the mind,
Endless wonders I shall find.
Thoughts like rivers flow and twist,
In shadows cast, I long to tryst.

Glances inward, brave and clear,
Bringing forth what I hold dear.
Whispers echo, memories call,
In this realm, I can have it all.

Each layer peeled, reveals a spark,
Of dreams once dimmed, now leave their mark.
Through tangled thoughts, I weave my quest,
Explorations deep, I find my rest.

In silence, I discover grace,
Hidden hopes, a warm embrace.
The journey made within the soul,
Can illuminate and make me whole.

So onward still, the path I tread,
To unearth treasures long since bled.
In explorations, I learn to thrive,
A world within, where I survive.

Downward Bound

With every step, the ground is near,
An urge to plunge, I feel no fear.
Gravity calls, a pull so strong,
Into the depths where I belong.

Downward bound, I drift and sway,
Through caverns dark, where shadows play.
The air grows thick, yet I press on,
To find the dawn after the dawn.

Stars above begin to fade,
As mysteries in darkness wade.
Caves that shelter dreams untold,
Echoing secrets, young and old.

Roots entangled, stories blend,
In the spiral where journeys end.
Each moment spent, a treasure gained,
In the quiet, I remain unchained.

So deep I wander, heart unbound,
In the depths of life where truths are found.
Downward bound, yet ever free,
The journey leads me back to me.

Chronicles of the Deep

In the depths where shadows play,
Whispers of the ocean sway.
Secrets hidden, tales unfold,
Memories of the brave and bold.

Tides remember ancient songs,
Where the pulse of water throngs.
Coral castles hold their breath,
Guardians of the dreams in death.

Creations swimming through the night,
Bioluminescent sparks of light.
Eternal dance beneath the waves,
Mysteries that the heart craves.

Echoes of a timeless lore,
Drifting through the ocean floor.
In silence deep, a story weaves,
Of shipwrecks, storms, and lost leaves.

Beneath the moon's gentle gaze,
Seashells cradle ancient ways.
Chronicles of the deep still call,
A siren's song to one and all.

Ancient Echoes

In the forest where echoes roam,
Whispers hint at a forgotten home.
Trees stand tall, their roots entwined,
Holding tales of the lost, maligned.

Beneath the canopy's green embrace,
Sunlight dances, a fleeting trace.
Leaves like pages, fluttering down,
In nature's book, old sorrows drown.

Stones remember the footsteps past,
Legends woven, shadows cast.
Ancient spirits sing their plea,
In the rustling leaves, wild and free.

Time stands still in the twilight glow,
Moments linger, softly flow.
The world holds its breath, then sighs,
As ancient echoes harmonize.

A tapestry of dreams unspooled,
In the heart of the woods, we're schooled.
Whisper your secrets, let them soar,
For ancient echoes live evermore.

Forgotten Passages

In labyrinths where shadows blend,
Lost paths stretch, they twist and bend.
Each turn hides a tale unknown,
Whispered soft in a faded tone.

Dusty tomes on every shelf,
Speak of journeys, quests of self.
Ink-stained secrets, stories thrum,
In forgotten passages, they hum.

Worn steps echo the dreams we seek,
Moments captured, silent, meek.
A journey through the sands of time,
In every corner, a rhyme.

Ghosts of travelers linger near,
Guardians of stories held dear.
They beckon softly, urge us forth,
To wander the paths, to seek our worth.

A treasure trove of hearts once brave,
In forgotten passages, we crave.
To hear the tales of those who came,
In every whisper, a lingering flame.

Flashes of Distant Light

In the night, the stars align,
Flickering flames in the vast design.
Each point a wish, a dream held tight,
Flashes of distant, shimmering light.

Across the void, a story calls,
Meandering through the cosmic halls.
Nebulas weave, galaxies spin,
Crafting a tapestry deep within.

Comets race with tails aglow,
Messengers from the heavens' flow.
Whispers carried on solar winds,
Of beginnings, journeys, and ends.

In twilight's grasp, we find our place,
As constellations dance with grace.
Illuminating paths unknown,
Flashes of light that guide us home.

The universe sings in radiant hues,
Every star a tale we choose.
In cosmos' embrace, we take flight,
Chasing the flashes of distant light.

A Quest for the Hidden

In valleys deep, where whispers dwell,
The secrets call, a silent bell.
With lantern's glow, we tread the ground,
In search of truths, yet to be found.

Through tangled roots and ancient stone,
We journey forth, not yet alone.
Each step reveals what shadows keep,
A hidden world, where secrets sleep.

The map unfolds, with ink of night,
Guiding us true, towards the light.
In every cave, a story breathes,
Of lives entwined among the leaves.

The echoes dance, with tales untold,
A treasure's worth, more than gold.
In every corner, whispers sigh,
Of dreams once lost, now soaring high.

Our quest, a thread, in time's vast loom,
Weaving fates, dispelling gloom.
With hearts ablaze, we seek and find,
The hidden realms, that shape mankind.

Echoes of the Underground

Beneath the surface, whispers flow,
In tunnels dark, where few will go.
The echoes call from depths unknown,
A symphony of stone and bone.

Through underground, we carve our way,
In shadows, night will turn to day.
Each heartbeat resonates, alive,
In caverns deep, where secrets thrive.

With every step, the silence grows,
A hidden world, where time slows.
The air is thick with ancient lore,
In echoes vast, we dare explore.

The past is woven in the walls,
In muted cries, the silence falls.
With every breath, a story's spun,
Of ages past, of battles won.

In echoes true, we find our peace,
In hidden realms, our hearts release.
The underground, a quiet friend,
Where journeys start, and never end.

Through the Earth's Embrace

In twilight's hush, the earth awaits,
With open arms, and whispered fates.
The depths below, a cradle tight,
In shadows soft, we find our light.

Each layer rich with tales of yore,
A tapestry of life's grand score.
With every touch, the soil hums,
Of all that grows, of all that comes.

We wander through the winding paths,
In nature's heart, we feel her baths.
The roots, like veins, connect us true,
To all that's past, and all that's new.

In caverns wide, the crystals gleam,
Reflecting hopes, and tangled dreams.
We trace our fingers on the stone,
In earthen hugs, we find our home.

Through earth's embrace, we shall remain,
In every loss, and every gain.
To seek the heart, where life aligns,
In sacred ground, our spirit shines.

Chasing Shadows Below

In twilight's grasp, the shadows creep,
Through hidden paths, where secrets sleep.
With each step down, we feel the pull,
Of whispered tales, both dark and full.

The lantern's light reveals the way,
To where the wild and forgotten play.
In corners damp, the silence sings,
Of buried hopes and lost old things.

Chasing shadows, we learn to see,
What lies behind, what's yet to be.
The stories etched in dusty air,
Of moments clasped, beyond compare.

With every turn, the darkness flows,
A dance of past, where mystery grows.
In every echo, we find our song,
Of where we've been, where we belong.

As shadows shift, the light will break,
A journey vast, we boldly take.
Through hidden realms, we shall explore,
In chasing shadows, we seek more.

In the Underworld Realm

Beneath the earth where shadows dwell,
A whisper rides the silent swell.
Darkness dances with a soft spun thread,
In the underworld, the lost are led.

Glimmers flicker in the deep abyss,
Voices echo, a forgotten kiss.
Ancient secrets in the stony clay,
Awaiting dawn to break the gray.

Serpents twist in a gentle sigh,
While the bones of the ancients lie.
Time stands still in this hidden keep,
Cradling dreams that forever sleep.

Flickers of light show paths to roam,
Guiding souls back to their home.
Eternal night in a solemn earth,
Holds the stories of life and birth.

Through the silence, hear the call,
Fallen empires, they rise and fall.
In the depths where the lost are found,
Life and death are tightly bound.

Chasms and Caverns

In chasms wide where echoes dwell,
A symphony of darkness swell.
Caverns deep with echoes loud,
Whispers weave through shadowed crowd.

Stalactites drip like thoughts of old,
Stories waiting to be told.
Ancient routes through paths unseen,
Guard the secrets of what has been.

Minerals shimmer, colors play,
In a world where sunlight strays.
Flickering lanterns seem to guide,
Lost adventurers through the tide.

Cracks and crevices form their hide,
In every corner, history's pride.
Those who wander must heed the sound,
For in silence, the truth is found.

Peering into the deep unknown,
Heartbeats of the earth are sown.
Chasms breathe with life anew,
In caverns dark, the ancient grew.

The Pulse Beneath

Beneath the crust, a heartbeat sings,
Echoes of life in hidden springs.
Vibrations hum through rock and clay,
Mapping tales of yesterday.

Every tremor, a story flows,
From depths unknown, the wisdom grows.
A rhythm pulsing, strong and bold,
Whispering secrets from the old.

In the silence, listen close,
To the heartbeat that we chose.
It beats with time, a tender tie,
Connecting earth to the vast sky.

Roots unravel, grasping deep,
In the soil where the ancients sleep.
The pulse beneath, a living art,
Binds the world, heart to heart.

Feel the thrum as shadows pass,
Through the fields of shimmering grass.
The earth's own song forever stays,
In the dance of life's sweet maze.

Roots of the Awakened

From the soil, tendrils rise,
Reaching forth beneath the skies.
Roots entwine in an ancient dance,
Whispering tales of fate and chance.

Awakened dreams from earth's embrace,
Finding comfort in this place.
Through the dark, they seek the light,
Striving onward, a hopeful sight.

Each root a story, rich and deep,
Harvested thoughts that we still keep.
In the curves of their gentle sway,
Time stands still, come what may.

Fields of green where spirits soar,
Life reborn, and yet, there's more.
Wind carries scents of days gone by,
As roots weave tales, never shy.

Embrace the earth beneath your feet,
Feel the life, so strong, so sweet.
For in this bond, we find our way,
Through roots of the awakened, we stay.

In Search of Distant Horizons

Beyond the hills where shadows play,
The sun dips down at the end of day.
Waves of whispers call my name,
To chase the dreams, to fuel the flame.

Across the fields where wildflowers bloom,
With every step, dispel the gloom.
A path unfolds with every breath,
An endless journey, defying death.

I wander far beyond the stars,
Past quiet lakes and ancient bars.
The horizon glimmers, just out of reach,
Lessons learned beyond what they teach.

Each moment holds a tale untold,
In every silence, secrets unfold.
To find my place, beneath the sky,
In search of horizons, I learn to fly.

In distant lands where dreams unite,
A tapestry woven with thread of light.
I'll chase the dawn with a hopeful heart,
For in the chase, life's true art.

Chasing the Inner Light

In the stillness, shadows creep,
A voice within stirs from sleep.
With every heartbeat, I must strive,
To find the glow that keeps me alive.

Through tangled thoughts and winding roads,
The essence of truth quietly erodes.
But in the silence, I hear it call,
The inner light that guides us all.

With eyes closed tight, I seek the flame,
A whisper soft, calling my name.
Illuminate the darkest parts,
Awakening dreams locked in our hearts.

In moments fraught with doubt and fear,
This inner light draws ever near.
It dances brightly, bold and free,
An echo of who I'm meant to be.

I chase the glimmer, heart held high,
Through storms and shadows, I will fly.
For every journey brings new insight,
A passage lit by the inner light.

Spiraling into the Depths

In shadows deep, where echoes fall,
I spiral down in whispered thrall.
Each step reveals a secret layer,
In depths unknown, I hold my prayer.

The pulse of earth beneath my feet,
In darkness beckons, bittersweet.
Through corridors of time and space,
I seek the truth amidst the trace.

With every heartbeat, shadows churn,
In fading light, my spirit yearns.
To understand the depth of night,
And draw from it a flicker of light.

In stillness found, the cave's embrace,
Unraveled fears in this quiet place.
To spiral further, I must be bold,
For in the depth, the truth unfolds.

This journey deep, a rite of soul,
Through swirling darkness, I become whole.
In every corner, shadows dance,
Spiraling into depths, I take my chance.

The Quest for Hidden Truths

Beneath the surface lies a spark,
A quest unfolds within the dark.
Whispers beckon on the breeze,
To uncover mysteries with ease.

In ancient tomes and silent signs,
The hidden truths, the sacred lines.
With open heart and mind sincere,
I seek the wisdom waiting near.

Through tangled paths and winding trails,
Each step reveals what seldom fails.
The world around, a puzzle vast,
In fragments clear, the future past.

Illusions fade as insights grow,
Unraveling tales time will bestow.
With every question comes the light,
To guide my heart into the night.

The quest continues, forever bright,
An endless journey towards the light.
For in the seeking, I find my way,
To hidden truths that softly sway.

Descent into the Unknown

Into the dark, we boldly tread,
Where shadows dance, and whispers spread.
The air is thick, with secrets cold,
A story ancient, yet untold.

With cautious steps, we move as one,
A journey to where light is none.
Each heartbeat echoes, a ghostly sound,
In this abyss, lost hopes surround.

The walls they close, the path they twist,
In every shadow, an unseen mist.
Fear grips tight, yet still we seek,
A glimmer, a spark, though we feel weak.

A flicker of truth, a sight of grace,
In the pitch of night, we find our place.
Through labyrinths deep, we wander far,
Chasing dreams beneath a distant star.

What will we find in this hollowed gloom?
A fate unknown, perhaps our doom.
Yet onward still, we brave the night,
For in the dark, we seek the light.

Whispers from the Underworld

From caverns deep, the voices rise,
Echoing softly, like mournful sighs.
Secrets linger in the cold damp air,
Whispers call from beyond despair.

A language lost, in shadows concealed,
The truth of ages, slowly revealed.
With bated breath, we lean in close,
To hear the tales that silence chose.

Each rustling leaf, each creak of stone,
Carries stories of the long-gone.
The past breathes here, in hushed tones,
Among the roots and ancient bones.

A chilling draft, a fleeting sound,
Within these depths, our hopes are bound.
We pen our fears on crumbling walls,
As silent specters weave their calls.

In this domain, where shadows dwell,
We unlock doors to heaven and hell.
Whispers turn to shouts, and we stand still,
Drawn deeper still by an iron will.

The Hidden Pathway

A narrow path, where few may go,
Beneath the earth, where roots entwine slow.
Here time is lost, and space is few,
A secret trove, where dreams come true.

The stones beneath hold stories old,
Of battles fought, of treasures told.
In twilight dim, we find our way,
A road less traveled, come what may.

Through winding turns, we wander deep,
In silence, ancient secrets keep.
The air is thick, with history's grace,
In every corner, a sacred place.

As lanterns flicker, shadows play,
Our hearts beat stronger, leading the way.
Each step a whisper, each breath a prayer,
On this hidden path, we find our share.

So onward we tread, through earth and stone,
In search of meaning, we are not alone.
This journey calls, with a gentle sway,
A hidden pathway, our souls' ballet.

Secrets of the Subterranean

Deep in the earth, where light won't go,
Lies a world unknown, cloaked in shadow.
The secrets there, in silence wait,
For those who dare to navigate.

With every step, we delve apply,
Unraveling tales where echoes lie.
In winding tunnels, history sings,
Of ancient kings, and forgotten things.

The ground beneath, a canvas worn,
Painted with stories, both joy and scorn.
Each crack and crevice tells a tale,
Of love and loss, of might and frail.

Through the darkness, our lantern glows,
Illuminating paths that no one knows.
We gather the whispers, like falling rain,
In this subterranean world, no pain.

And so we go, hand in hand,
Discovering truths like grains of sand.
In the heart of earth, we find our fate,
Secrets of the subterranean, destined to await.

Beneath the Surface: A Tale

In quiet depths where secrets sleep,
A world resides, its silence deep.
Whispers of waves, a gentle sway,
Lost stories linger, drift away.

Fish weave tales through coral halls,
Ancient echoes in soothing calls.
Sunlight dances, glimmers bright,
A ballet of shadows, pure delight.

Beneath the waves, life takes its breath,
Canvas painted, a vibrant depth.
Mysteries bloom, in currents flow,
Nature's secrets, hidden below.

Each ripple holds a story untold,
A pirate's treasure, a sailor's gold.
Tales of love and battles past,
In the embrace of the sea, they last.

Beneath the surface, dreams reside,
In ocean's arms, where hearts abide.
With every tide, new tales arise,
A tapestry woven beneath our skies.

The Cradle of Silence

In whispers soft, the night descends,
A cradle where the quiet bends.
Moonlight spills on dreams unspooled,
In stillness, all the fears are cooled.

Stars like guardians, watch the scene,
Holding secrets, pure and keen.
Silhouettes of memories glide,
In this haven, hopes abide.

Each breath a lullaby in disguise,
A haven where the heart can rise.
The pulse of night, a rhythmic sigh,
Cradled softly, time drifts by.

Shadows dance on velvet skies,
Like fleeting dreams and whispered lies.
Underneath, a world awaits,
To cradle life as it creates.

In silence bound, the dawn will break,
A new chapter for hope's sake.
Cradle of silence, pure and bright,
Where dreams unfold in softest light.

Foundations of the Deep

Beneath the waves, the earth does sigh,
Where stories merge and shadows lie.
Roots of time in tangled weave,
Echoes of what we believe.

Coral structures rise like towers,
A kingdom built through sun's sweet hours.
Endless cycles ebb and flow,
Life's foundations, deep below.

Currents carve and shape the land,
With gentle force, they understand.
Nature's sculptor, patient, wise,
Building dreams beneath the skies.

In caverns vast, a world unfolds,
Of ancient giants and tales retold.
Every stone, a chapter penned,
Foundation strong, on which we depend.

In unity, the depths connect,
Life's vast puzzle, we reflect.
From foundations deep, we take our part,
In this vast journey, heart to heart.

Beneath the Layers of Time

In gentle folds, the past resides,
Like whispered secrets, time confides.
Layers stack like pages worn,
Stories lost, yet still reborn.

Each stratum holds a life once lived,
A testament to all that's given.
Memories enveloped, soft and real,
In every touch, the past can heal.

Time, a river, flows and bends,
Creating beauty as it ascends.
Beneath the surface, roots run deep,
Where echoes of history gently seep.

Embrace the moments, fleeting fast,
In layers thick, remember the past.
Each heartbeat echoes, a gentle chime,
Beneath the layers, we dance with time.

In every glance, a story's trace,
The beauty found in fleeting grace.
As we unearth what's left behind,
We find our way, hearts intertwined.

The Heart of the Earth

Deep below the forest's shade,
Whispers of the roots cascade.
In the soil, secrets thrive,
Nature's pulse, alive, alive.

Crystals gleam in caves so dark,
Shadows dance, igniting spark.
Beneath the hills, in silence deep,
Earth's warm heart, its dreams to keep.

Mountains sigh with ancient grace,
Valleys cradle time and space.
Through the earth, we journey far,
Finding light in every scar.

Voices of the past resound,
In this haven, truth is found.
Roots and stones, they intertwine,
Whispering tales, divine design.

With every step, we learn and grow,
In the depth, our spirits flow.
The heart of earth, so rich and wide,
In its embrace, we shall abide.

Subterranean Dreams

Beneath the surface, dreams ignite,
In hidden realms, they take flight.
Mossy carpets, shadows play,
Time slips gently, night and day.

Echoes murmur, secrets speak,
In this world, we seldom peek.
Crystal waters, silent streams,
Flowing softly, weaving dreams.

Creatures roam in twilight's hush,
In the depths, there's little rush.
Fading echoes of laughter ring,
In the dark, the soul takes wing.

Stories etched in stone and dust,
Trust the journey, learn to trust.
Through the layers, life unfolds,
In the chill, the warmth it holds.

Beneath the world we thought we knew,
An unseen tapestry, so true.
Subterranean whispers call,
In their depths, we find it all.

Into the Abyss

Eyes wide open, step on down,
Into the abyss, without a frown.
Lost in shadows, depths unknown,
In the silence, we have grown.

The air feels thick, the darkness stirs,
Whispers haunting, heart of fur.
Rivers of thought, currents guide,
Into the void, where truth resides.

Bubbles rise, a breath of light,
Illuminating the endless night.
Every heartbeat, deeper still,
Facing fears, bending will.

What lies beneath is yet to see,
An endless dance of mystery.
Into the abyss, we fall and fly,
In realms where fears and hopes all lie.

In this embrace, we find our fate,
Chaos and calm, we meditate.
In the abyss, we redefine,
The edges of shadow and light entwine.

Layers of Existence

In the layers of existence, we dive,
Seeking truths that help us thrive.
From the surface, we peel away,
Unveiling dreams that softly sway.

Beneath the chaos, calm resides,
In each heartbeat, the world abides.
Life's fabric woven, multiple strands,
Intertwined like ancient bands.

Every layer tells a tale,
Of joy, of sorrow, of winds that wail.
Peering down through time's great lens,
Discovering how each soul amends.

Colors blend in vibrant hue,
In layers, we find the ever new.
Moments captured, then set free,
In this dance of complexity.

From earth to sky, we stretch and reach,
In this maze, there's much to teach.
Layers of existence, rich and profound,
In every heartbeat, life's beauty found.

Hidden Realms of Wonder

In forests green, where secrets hide,
Whispers dance with the ebbing tide.
Beneath the trees, in shadows deep,
Enchanting dreams begin to creep.

A glimmer sparkles in the night,
As starlit paths come into sight.
The moonlight weaves a silver veil,
And tells the tale of nightingale.

Winding trails of magic flow,
Through ancient woods, where wildflowers grow.
A chorus calls from depths unknown,
Where every heart finds a hidden home.

With every step, the wonders call,
In hidden realms, we can have it all.
We chase the dreams in twilight's glow,
In nature's arms, we come to know.

Deep Underground Odyssey

Beneath the earth, where shadows loom,
A world awakens from the gloom.
With hidden paths and ancient stone,
The whispers of the past are sown.

Tunnels carved by time's own hand,
Lead us to a forgotten land.
Where echoes of the ages sing,
In darkness, hope begins to spring.

Mysterious roots entwine and weave,
A tale that few can hope to leave.
Through caverns wide with glimmering light,
Adventure waits in the quiet night.

Crystal lakes and rivers flow,
In depths where only brave hearts go.
Each hidden nook a story tells,
Deep underground, where magic dwells.

Subterranean Chronicles

In earthen chambers, secrets lie,
Beneath the sky, where shadows sigh.
A chronicle etched in rock so old,
Of stories lost, and dreams retold.

Through winding caves, we journey deep,
Among the silence, mysteries sleep.
Each corner turned, the past ignites,
As history whispers through the nights.

The drip of water sings its tune,
In caverns bright beneath the moon.
With every step, we feel the weight,
Of ages past, and threads of fate.

Crystals glisten, a radiant glow,
Guiding us where few dare to go.
In subterranean tales unwind,
New worlds await, our hearts aligned.

Inside the Crust

Beneath the surface, layers unfold,
Inside the crust, tales yet untold.
Where magma flows and roots entwine,
The heart of earth, so vast, divine.

In fissures deep, the secrets dwell,
Of creation's breath, a silent spell.
We uncover truths, both fierce and fair,
Inside the crust, we breathe the air.

Ancient rocks in silence stand,
Bearing witness to nature's hand.
Through fractured walls and hidden seams,
A world exists beyond our dreams.

Buried treasures, stories lost,
Remind us always of the cost.
With every journey, we shall find,
The pulse of earth, forever kind.

In Pursuit of the Depths

In the shadows where silence dwells,
Whispers echo of ancient spells.
Beneath the waves, secrets hide,
In the dark, old truths abide.

Waves crash down, a rhythm profound,
Pulling me deep, where wonders are found.
Fishes dance in the liquid embrace,
As I dive deeper, losing all trace.

Time stands still in the ocean's heart,
With every breath, I drift and depart.
Coral reefs, like castles of light,
Guard the depths, both wondrous and bright.

The weight of the water, a lover's hold,
Tales of the sea that must be told.
In pursuit of the depths, I lose control,
Yet find in the journey, the essence of soul.

A Descent into Mystery

Through the mist, a path unwinds,
Leading to realms where thought unbinds.
Each step cloaked in a shroud of lore,
As shadows beckon from yonder shore.

Echoes linger, with a story to tell,
Of dreams and fears woven in spell.
A descent into the heart of night,
Where darkness reveals its hidden light.

Bridges built from whispers and sighs,
Carrying hopes up to the skies.
In this realm of flickering doubt,
The draws of silence softly shout.

With each heartbeat, a mystery grows,
A dance of shadows beneath the throes.
In the unknown, there's beauty to seek,
A descent into the depths, oh so sleek.

The Pulse of the Planet

In every heartbeat, the earth exhales,
The mountains listen, the ocean wails.
Rhythms of nature, so pure and spry,
The pulse of the planet, a lullaby.

Seeds sown deep in the fertile ground,
Life awakens with a joyous sound.
The forests whisper, in a vibrant choir,
Singing tales that never tire.

Beneath the surface, currents run,
A dance of power, yet so undone.
In every rustle, the stories unfold,
Of battles fought, and champions bold.

The pulse of the planet beats with grace,
Each creature finds its rightful place.
Connection flows like rivers wide,
In every heart, the earth's pride.

Unraveling Roots

In tangled webs where stories weave,
Ancient roots beneath believe.
They whisper soft, of times gone past,
Of love and loss, shadows cast.

Through the soil, their tendrils creep,
In hidden realms where secrets sleep.
Branches reaching, yearning for light,
In every shadow, a flicker of bright.

Unraveling threads of life and lore,
A tapestry rich, forever to explore.
Memories held in every grain,
Of laughter, sorrow, joy, and pain.

Roots intertwined, a dance so old,
Stories exchanged, like treasures of gold.
In their embrace, I find my place,
Connecting to earth, with endless grace.

Entryways to the Unknown

In shadows deep, the doors await,
With whispers soft, they seal our fate.
Each creak and groan, a tale to tell,
Of paths unseen, of secrets held.

Glimmers faint, through cracks of time,
A restless heart, begins to climb.
The air is thick, with dreams obscure,
What lies beyond, we can't be sure.

Footsteps echo, in hallways long,
Through veils of mist, where we belong.
Each voice a thread, in tapestry,
Woven with care, yet wild and free.

Expectations fade, like dawn's first light,
In corners dark, we find our sight.
The world expands, with every step,
Into the void, our spirits leapt.

So take a breath, and cross that line,
Into the realms where shadows shine.
With open hearts and open eyes,
We'll dance with fate, 'neath unknown skies.

Voyages Underfoot

Each pebble tells, a story worn,
Of tides and winds, of dreams reborn.
They guide our path, with whispered lore,
Beneath our feet, the world explores.

The cracks in stone, the earth's embrace,
Hold history vast, in every place.
We wander paths, of ancient trails,
Where roots entwined, tell silent tales.

A river bends, its course undone,
In mirrored depths, reflections run.
We step with care, on fragile ground,
In nature's grip, our hearts are bound.

Through fields of green, or desert's haze,
Each journey molds, our lives ablaze.
From sacred earth, to mountains high,
The planet sings, beneath the sky.

So take a step, with weightless grace,
In every footprint, find your place.
For every path, however slight,
Leads us to joy, or to the light.

Subsurface Fables

Beneath the soil, the stories seed,
Of life unseen, where roots proceed.
They twist and turn, in darkness deep,
With secrets held, in timeless sleep.

In caverns cool, where echoes beat,
The pulse of earth, our hearts repeat.
The whispers weave, of lore untold,
Of shadows long, and dreams of old.

The creatures crawl, in silent night,
While stars above, shine ever bright.
Each movement stirs, the ancient dust,
In realms of earth, we place our trust.

Through tunnels vast, and winding ways,
We find our peace, in nature's gaze.
The underground hum, a song so pure,
In every crack, a hope to cure.

So let us delve, into the night,
Discover wealth, in darkened light.
Subsurface fables, waiting there,
For hearts that dare, to dream and share.

Beneath the Horizon

The sky unfolds, a canvas wide,
With colors bright, the world's tide.
Yet under waves, the stories flow,
Beneath the horizon, what do we know?

In depths unseen, the secrets dance,
Where time doth bend, to circumstance.
Coral castles, with whispers loud,
In currents soft, they drift like clouds.

Each creature swims, with purpose bold,
In oceans deep, where mysteries hold.
Beneath the surface, life ignites,
In realms of blue, with endless sights.

The sun dips low, in fiery grace,
While shadows play, they find their place.
The horizon beckons, we chase the light,
Into the depths, from day to night.

So venture forth, with heart so true,
To realms beneath, where dreams break through.
For in the depths, we come alive,
Beneath the horizon, we learn to thrive.

Veins of the Earth

Beneath the soil, life flows deep,
Silent currents, secrets to keep.
Roots intertwine in a dance divine,
Holding the tales of every vine.

Mountains rise, where shadows play,
The heartbeat of nature, night and day.
Rivers carve paths in a gentle grace,
Winds whisper softly, nature's embrace.

Fossils linger, stories unfold,
History's whispers, treasures untold.
Veins of the earth, solid and true,
Connecting us all, me and you.

Through ages past, the world has spun,
Each layer speaks of what's been done.
In every crack and every seam,
Lies the essence of a dream.

From depths unknown to heights unseen,
Nature's art, vibrant and green.
Veins of the earth, alive and bright,
A timeless wonder, pure delight.

Submerged Whispers

Beneath the waves, silenced cries,
Echoing truths in muted sighs.
Fathoms hide the dreams we seek,
In darkness deep, the oceans speak.

Coral castles guard their realms,
Where sunbeams dance and silence helms.
Tides cradle tales of ships long lost,
In whispered legends, we count the cost.

Fish dart like thoughts in watery space,
In tranquil depths, they find their grace.
Submerged whispers of love and despair,
Secrets entwined, flowing in air.

The moon pulls gently at every heart,
As currents weave a mystic art.
Bubbles rise to share a dream,
While shadows flicker, dance, and gleam.

In the silence, life ebbs and flows,
Unveiling wonders only nature knows.
Submerged whispers, serene and deep,
Hold the stories the oceans keep.

The Path Beneath

Beneath our feet, the stories lie,
Ancient paths where shadows sigh.
Roots that twist and branches spread,
Whispers of those, who've long since fled.

Footsteps echo on cobblestone,
Love and loss in every tone.
Hidden trails, kissed by the night,
Guide the wanderers in soft light.

The crunch of leaves, the rustle of grass,
Memories woven that never pass.
Each turn reveals a life's embrace,
Timeless journeys in every place.

Through tangled woods and meadows wide,
Nature's heartbeat is our guide.
The path beneath, a sacred thread,
Binding us to all who've tread.

Stars above, a guiding flame,
Tracing back to where we came.
In every step, a tale retold,
The path beneath, a treasure bold.

Echoes from Below

In caverns deep, the echoes call,
Whispers of time, both big and small.
A world unseen, where shadows blend,
Where darkened corners never end.

Footsteps linger on ancient stone,
In silence found, hearts feel alone.
Stalactites drip like a teardrop's fall,
A symphony played in nature's hall.

The pulse of earth, a steady beat,
Where all of life's rhythms meet.
Echoes from below, soft and clear,
Carrying hopes, dispelling fear.

Mysterious depths, secrets unfold,
Each whisper a tale, new and old.
In tunnels vast, the past resides,
Echoes from below, where truth hides.

And though we climb to reach the sky,
The earth below will never lie.
In echoes soft, we find our way,
To brighter dawns and fading day.

A Passage to the Unexplored

In whispered winds the secrets lie,
A path that leads where shadows sigh,
Through forests dense with tales untold,
We venture forth, both brave and bold.

A river's song, a beckoning flow,
With every step, the mysteries grow,
The heart beats loud, the spirit calls,
As twilight dances through the halls.

Beyond the hills, the skies expand,
In realms untouched, we take our stand,
For in the night, the stars align,
In every pulse, we seek a sign.

Yet doubts may rise like misty fears,
Through darkened paths, we shed our tears,
But with each challenge, we embrace,
The journey's worth, the wild's grace.

The unexplored, a siren's song,
In every step, we feel we belong,
Through ancient woods, and mountains high,
A passage awaits beneath the sky.

The Enigma Below

Beneath the earth, in silence deep,
Where shadows linger, secrets keep,
The pulse of ages, softly hums,
An enigma calls, as darkness comes.

Caves adorned with crystal light,
Where time dissolves, and none take flight,
The echoes whisper, tales of old,
In depths unseen, the brave are bold.

With every step, the silence grows,
An ancient world that none yet knows,
The heartbeat of the earth below,
In hidden paths, our dreams shall flow.

Yet fear may creep in fragile minds,
As mysteries hide, what truth unwinds?
But still we venture, drawn to seek,
The stories buried, the truths we speak.

The enigma waits in shadows cast,
With open hearts, we leave the past,
For in the dark, we find our light,
A journey deep, a wild flight.

Roots of the Rising Dawn

From soil rich, new futures sprout,
In tender light, we work it out,
The roots grow deep, their grip is strong,
With every dawn, we sing our song.

Through trials faced and lessons learned,
The heart ignites, the spirit burned,
In unity, we take our stand,
Together bound, we join our hand.

And as the sun breaks through the grey,
The world awakens, finds its way,
A vibrant hue, the skies adorn,
The roots emerge, from night to morn.

Hope rises high, like blossoms bright,
In the embrace of morning light,
With every step, we forge anew,
The dreams we weave, the paths we pursue.

In roots we trust, in dreams we grow,
From every challenge, strength will flow,
For in the dawn, our spirits soar,
The rising sun opens the door.

Explorations in the Dark

In shadows cast, we find our way,
Through whispered fears, we seek the play,
The night unfolds with mystery's embrace,
In darkened realms, we find our place.

With lanterns bright, we chase the night,
Each flicker spark, a guiding light,
As stars above begin to gleam,
The paths unveil our wildest dream.

Yet doubts may linger in the air,
A haunting chill, a whispered prayer,
But courage blooms where shadows lie,
In explorations, we learn to fly.

Through tangled woods and echoes deep,
The treasures lie for those who leap,
With open hearts, our spirits flare,
In every journey, nothing rare.

The dark will fade, as dawn appears,
We've conquered doubts, we've faced our fears,
In explorations, life unfolds,
A tapestry woven in tales of old.

Depths of the Unseen

In shadows deep where secrets sleep,
Whispers trail the silent deep.
Beneath the waves, the lost will creep,
In dreams, their haunting echoes leap.

The ocean's heart, a pulse concealed,
Mysteries in darkness healed.
Untold tales, like pearls revealed,
In depths where time has never squealed.

A universe of liquid night,
In currents strong, we lose our sight.
Yet in the dark, there lives a light,
A song of souls that takes to flight.

Titanic beasts in shadows play,
Their laughter lost in disarray.
A fragile dance in tides' ballet,
Eternal rhythms guide their sway.

We seek to chart those spaces vast,
But wave and tide have secrets cast.
In every depth, a story passed,
In ocean's womb, our dreams amassed.

A Voyage Beneath the Surface

Upon the skin of water's glass,
Adventurers sail as moments pass.
With every wave, dreams fill the mass,
Of journeys taken through the brass.

A compass points to paths unknown,
As treasures lie where light has shone.
Through azure realms, our hearts have grown,
In depths of blue, we find our throne.

The fish weave tales of epochs long,
In bubbles forged from silent song.
The currents carry us along,
To places where the brave belong.

From ship to tide, the dance begins,
Each splash a challenge, each wave spins.
In every storm, it's here love wins,
For in the depths, our story sins.

Beneath the surface, life is bold,
In shadows deep, true gems unfold.
The ocean whispers, secrets told,
Of voyages unclaimed, yet gold.

Echoes from the Core

In caves of stone where echoes roam,
Whispers rise like smoke to comb.
The language born of earth and loam,
A memory's sigh, a distant home.

From deep within, a tremor calls,
Through silence thick, the caverns thrall.
Each pulse of time, the ancients brawl,
In rhythmic beats, the shadows fall.

The heart of earth, a steady drum,
In chambers dark, where shadows come.
Each echo leads to where we're from,
An ancient dance, alive, and numb.

When fissures break and sunlight streams,
A symphony of hidden dreams.
The core of life, or so it seems,
Awakens us to endless themes.

So listen close, let echoes weave,
A tale of life we dare believe.
In every breath, a chance to grieve,
And rise again, as souls conceive.

Labyrinth of the Heart

In twisted paths where shadows play,
The heart's deep maze leads us astray.
Each turn unveils what words can't say,
In whispers lost, we find our way.

Amidst the walls, a truth resides,
In corridors where love abides.
With every heartbeat, fate collides,
A tempest fierce, where hope confides.

The echoes bounce from stone to stone,
The memories of hands once sewn.
In every corner, seeds are sown,
Of laughter shared, of dreams outgrown.

Yet as we wander through the night,
The labyrinth reveals its light.
For every shadow, there's a bright,
A passage leading to what's right.

So navigate with tender grace,
In every turn, find a new place.
For in the heart, life leaves a trace,
Of all the love we dare embrace.

Earthbound Reveries

In fields of green where whispers play,
The sun dips low, end of the day.
Soft breezes carry dreams to flight,
In the warming glow of fading light.

Beneath the trees where shadows creep,
Nature sings her song so deep.
A melody of winds and leaves,
In every hush, the heart believes.

As stars awaken in the night,
Their twinkling eyes, a pure delight.
They tell of worlds yet to explore,
Beyond the hills, from shore to shore.

With every sigh, the earth will breathe,
A whispered sigh, it will bequeath.
The dreams of those who walk her land,
In unity, we take our stand.

So let us dance on soil and stone,
In every step, we find our own.
With hearts aligned and spirits free,
Together, bound in harmony.

Into Twilight's Embrace

The dusk arrives, a gentle shroud,
Where echoes fade, and shadows crowd.
The sky, ablaze with hues so rare,
Invites the stars with tender care.

Within this realm where day departs,
The silent call of hidden hearts.
Against the twilight's velvet fold,
New tales of wonder soon unfold.

A quiet path through whispering trees,
Where secrets linger in the breeze.
This moment, fleeting yet profound,
Is where our lost dreams can be found.

In twilight's light, we catch a glimpse,
Of fleeting shadows with their prints.
They guide us gently through the night,
To realms of solace, pure delight.

So let us wander hand in hand,
On this enchanted, timeless land.
For in the twilight's warm embrace,
We find our peace, our sacred space.

A Tapestry of Depths

In oceans vast, where shadows dwell,
The secrets lie, too deep to tell.
Each wave a story, whispered low,
A dance of currents, ebb and flow.

From coral beds to kelp so tall,
Life weaves a pattern, interrawl.
A tapestry of vibrant hues,
In every thread, the ocean's muse.

The rhythm of the tides, they sing,
A song of life, in every spring.
From creatures small to giants great,
United here, by fate's own bait.

Beneath the surface, worlds collide,
A universe in which we hide.
We seek understanding, wisdom's depth,
In nature's grasp, our spirits swept.

So let us dive and seek the light,
In depths of blue, beyond the night.
For in the ocean's warm embrace,
We find our truth, our sacred place.

Beneath the Starry Veil

At nightfall's door, the stars awake,
A cosmic dance, they softly make.
They twinkle bright, like dreams unfurled,
Guiding us through the vast, cool world.

Beneath this veil, our hopes take flight,
In silken threads of shimmering light.
Each star, a wish, a whispered chance,
We feel their pull, inviting dance.

From distant suns to moons that glow,
The universe reveals its flow.
With every glance, horizons blend,
In starlit whispers, hearts transcend.

In quiet moments, we are one,
Beneath the arch of night undone.
The cosmos calls, we hear its plea,
In silent vows, we learn to be.

So drift among the glowing skies,
As constellations guide our sighs.
For under this celestial dome,
We find our path, we find our home.

Beyond the Surface Glare

Beneath the sunlit flow, we hide,
Tales of whispers, currents wide.
Secrets woven in the tide,
In the shadows, dreams abide.

Glimmers dance on rippling waves,
Memories of ancient graves.
Voices call through the silent spaces,
In the depths, time embraces.

A shimmer hints at the unknown,
Yearning hearts that have been grown.
Beneath the laughter, pain is sown,
Where hope and despair have flown.

Tides may ebb, yet still they flow,
With every surge, the stories grow.
In the stillness, truths will show,
A journey deeper than we know.

So dare to dive beyond the hue,
Find the essence, find what's true.
In water's kiss, we find our view,
Beyond the surface, dreams renew.

Eyes Toward the Ground

Where footsteps tread on earth and stone,
The heart finds solace, not alone.
In every crack, a tale is sewn,
Beneath the weight of seeds once thrown.

Eyes cast downward, gaze on fate,
In humble paths, we contemplate.
Among the roots that intertwine,
A world below, both dark and fine.

Fingers trace the sacred dirt,
Awakened hearts where silence flirts.
From every grain, a voice will rise,
In nature's grasp, the spirit flies.

Yet heads must lift to skies so blue,
But first, we honor what is true.
For hidden gems in soil do gleam,
And shape our paths, a shared dream.

So wander low, and find the sound,
In all that's lost beneath the ground.
There's wisdom found where roots are bound,
In humble places, life is crowned.

Within the Silent Caverns

Echoes linger in the dark,
Whispers soft, a hidden spark.
Drip of water, pulse of stone,
In silent chambers, time is grown.

Shadows dance on ancient walls,
Nature's breath in quiet calls.
Secrets told by each cold breeze,
In hushed repose, the heart finds ease.

Footsteps light on gravel floors,
Past the myths, the lore restores.
Every stalactite tells a tale,
Of journeys taken, trails so frail.

While daylight fades above the earth,
In darkness blooms a sacred birth.
Stars of stone, they shine and guide,
Within the caverns, we confide.

So venture deep, through darkness roam,
In silent caves, the soul finds home.
With every echo, wisdom blooms,
In quiet depths, dispel the glooms.

Odyssey of the Undercurrent

Beneath the waves, a current swirls,
Whispers hidden, secrets unfurl.
In shadows deep, the wanderers glide,
In quiet places, hope and pride.

With every push, the water speaks,
In silent depths, the heart still seeks.
Roots entwined in the ocean's heart,
Each undertow plays its part.

With kelp and shells, a dance begins,
The rhythm of life, where silence wins.
In the undercurrent, a story flows,
Of ancient tides and ebbing woes.

Bubbles rise to break the still,
As life beneath begins to thrill.
Flashes of light, a fleeting glance,
In the watery realm, we take a chance.

So dive into the depths of dreams,
Where every current softly teems.
An odyssey beneath the skin,
In the undercurrent, life will spin.

Mysteries of the Buried

Whispers of secrets lie in the ground,
Echoes of stories that never resound.
Roots clasp the past in their tangled embrace,
Shadows of time in a hidden space.

Bones of forgotten, in silence they stay,
Guardians of dreams that have faded away.
Lost in the silence where memories linger,
Tales of the ancients slip through each finger.

Rusty old keys in a chest out of sight,
Unlocking the darkness, reclaiming the light.
Each grain of the earth holds a fragment of hope,
Weaving the fabric of life's fragile kaleidoscope.

Beneath ancient stones lies a world unexplored,
Legacies buried, in silence adored.
Time turns the pages of history's tome,
Each layer a heartbeat, a piece of our home.

With every dig deeper, a truth to behold,
The whispers of ages, a tale to be told.
Emerging from shadows, the past intertwines,
Mysteries buried, where time redefines.

Sculpted by Darkness

In shadows we carve what the light cannot see,
Figures emerge from the void, wild and free.
Chiseled by night, with a delicate grace,
Dancing through whispers in a soft, silent space.

Every contour speaks of forgotten lore,
Stories unspoken, reaching for more.
Sculpted by darkness, where dreams intertwine,
Molding the essence of the line between time.

Figures twist softly, in fluid embrace,
Shadows become canvas, a celestial place.
Lines etched in silence, alive in the night,
Crafted with care, glowing from within light.

The art of the unseen, where echoes refrain,
Through halls of the night, our spirits remain.
In the depths of dark, where secrets abide,
Sculpted by shadows, the heart's open wide.

And so in this realm, we dance with our fears,
Creating a beauty that transcends our years.
For in every darkness, a form must appear,
Sculpted by silence, born from the seer.

Into the Deep Enigma

Beneath the surface, the mysteries pulse,
Whispers of currents pull us like a waltz.
Into the deep, where the shadows conspire,
Secrets awaken, igniting desire.

Echoes of legends drift through the foam,
Ancient mariners calling us home.
Each wave a question, each swell a refrain,
Drawing us closer through ebb and through strain.

The depths hold allure and a shiver of fear,
Treasures forgotten, their stories unclear.
Every dive deeper, a heart's wild critique,
Into the vastness, the soul feels antique.

In caverns of water, where sunlight can't reach,
Hidden in silence, dark wisdom will teach.
Crystals of time, glimmer softly in gloom,
Guiding the wanderers seeking their doom.

With every descent, we unravel the knot,
Finding the answers that once were forgot.
Into the deep, the enigma unfolds,
A tale of the ocean, in silence it holds.

In Search of the Underbelly

Beneath the surface, the world lies below,
A hidden expanse where shadows can grow.
In search of the underbelly's embrace,
Discovering truths in a secret space.

Layers unseen, where the roots intertwine,
Binding the stories of ages in line.
Pulsing with life, yet cloaked in disguise,
Veins of the earth drawing dreams through the skies.

The heart of the earth beats in rhythms unknown,
Sculpted by forces, in silence they've grown.
Cracks in the surface, a call to explore,
Unearthing the wonders that lie at our core.

Echoes of movement, the beat of the land,
Beliefs long forgotten, a history grand.
With every step taken, we delve into lore,
In search of the underbelly's core.

As night drapes its mantle, the shadows ignite,
The depths beckon softly, inviting the night.
In search of the underbelly, the journey unfolds,
Ancient and sacred, a treasure of old.

The Great Descent

Into the shadows, whispers creep,
Echoes linger, secrets keep.
Downward spirals, heartbeats race,
In the void, we find our place.

Gravity pulls with silent might,
Guiding souls into the night.
Lost in dreams, we start to fall,
Brave the depths, answer the call.

A tapestry woven with despair,
Yet hope glimmers in the air.
Through the dark, a flicker shines,
Reminding us of hidden signs.

Each tear nourishes the ground,
In silence, strength can be found.
From the depths, we rise anew,
Transformed by all we've been through.

With every challenge that we face,
We carve our path, we leave our trace.
The great descent, a journey grand,
Together we stand, hand in hand.

Terrain of Tales Untold

In the valley where shadows meet,
Stories linger beneath our feet.
Mountains whisper ancient lore,
Echoes of triumph, tales of war.

Winding rivers carve their way,
Carrying voices of yesterday.
Each stone and stream bears witness true,
To the journeys of me and you.

Endless skies paint colors bold,
In every hue, a tale unfolds.
The tales of love, the songs of strife,
Written in the fabric of life.

Amongst the trees, stories breathe,
In every leaf, new dreams we weave.
From sunrise glow to twilight's rest,
This terrain, a true heart's quest.

Together we wander, together we roam,
In the stories of others, we find our home.
A rich tapestry, woven with care,
In the terrain of tales, we all share.

Illuminating the Deep

Beneath the waves, a world awaits,
In shadows play the curious fates.
Glimmers dance where darkness thrives,
In the deep, the mystery lives.

Coral gardens, vibrant and bright,
Home to creatures of pure delight.
Silent whispers call from below,
In this realm, our spirits flow.

Amidst the currents, life intertwines,
Every heartbeat, a story shines.
With each ripple, the ocean sings,
Unlocking the magic that living brings.

In the elusive, lessons unfold,
Teaching us to be brave and bold.
Illuminated by the depths we trust,
Embracing the journey, return to dust.

From light above to darkened sea,
Unity flows through you and me.
Illuminating tales of dark and deep,
In the silence, our secrets keep.

Beneath Brighter Skies

Under the vast and endless blue,
Dreams take flight, emotions true.
Each cloud whispers of what could be,
Beneath brighter skies, we feel free.

Promises dwell in the gentle breeze,
Softly carrying hopes with ease.
In the laughter of the trees,
Nature's song, a sweet reprise.

With every sunrise, a chance anew,
To chase the dreams that feel so true.
In every sunset, colors paint,
A reminder that life can be quaint.

Together we dance in the golden light,
Finding our way through day and night.
Beneath brighter skies, our spirits soar,
In the embrace of the world we adore.

Each moment cherished, a memory made,
In the glow of life, we are unafraid.
Beneath the vastness, hearts intertwine,
In this journey, together we shine.

Whispers from Below

In shadows deep, where echoes creep,
The whispers call, secrets to keep.
From ancient soil, tales intertwined,
A silent song, in darkness defined.

Through cracks of stone, the voices rise,
Soft murmurs weave 'neath midnight skies.
They speak of dreams once lost to time,
In forgotten places, they rhyme.

In depths of earth, their stories bloom,
A distant past that breaks the gloom.
With every sigh, a journey starts,
Guiding the weary, mending hearts.

Oh, listen close, the tales they bring,
Of loves once bright, now shadows cling.
Beneath the weight of years gone by,
The whispers linger, never die.

Roots of the Ancient

Beneath the trees, where silence reigns,
The roots run deep, binding like chains.
In earth's embrace, their secrets lie,
A tapestry woven, reaching high.

With every twist, a story grows,
Of ages past and nature's flows.
In whispered wind, their voices merge,
The ancient call, a primal urge.

From seed to tree, in shadows cast,
The wisdom waits, connected fast.
Their strength unseen, yet ever true,
A lifeline drawn between the two.

Watch closely now, as branches sway,
The roots below hold night and day.
In every leaf, a secret shared,
The ancient speaks, for those who dared.

Concealed Tales

Behind the masks, the tales reside,
In every heart, a place to hide.
The secrets kept, from light of day,
In shadows whispered, they sway.

With eyes that see beyond the veil,
They draw us close, their stories frail.
In every nook, and cranny small,
A world unknown awaits the call.

From whispered vows to broken dreams,
The truth unfolds in silent streams.
Each tale a thread, intricately spun,
In solitude, they come undone.

So search the depths, the hidden door,
For every tale holds something more.
In quiet moments, let thoughts sail,
Discover here the concealed tales.

The Buried Odyssey

Beneath the sands, the journeys lie,
In whispers low, where moments die.
Each grain a fragment of the past,
A tale untold, waiting to clasp.

Through ancient ruins, the stories weave,
Of those who loved, and those who grieve.
In echoes soft, their footsteps roam,
In every heartbeat, they find a home.

From distant lands, the paths entwined,
An odyssey that fate designed.
The sun-kissed shores where dreams set sail,
In every wave, the whispers trail.

So dig through earth, and feel the pulse,
Of journeys marked by life's convulse.
A buried odyssey, waiting near,
In layers deep, the past appears.

9 781805 616214